Mission Can Be Fun!

Barry Osborne

Rural Mission Solutions
Centre for Rural Mission
4 Clarence Street
Market Harborough
LE16 7NE
www.ruralmissionsolutions.org.uk
Telephone 01858 414930

Copyright © 2020 Rural Mission Solutions

Published in 2020

The right of Barry Osborne to be identified as the Author of this Work has been asserted by him in accordance with the Copyright, Designs and Patents Act 1988.

All rights reserved. No part of this publication may be reproduced, stored in a retrieval system or transmitted, in any form or by any means, without the prior written permission of the publisher.

ISBN: 978-1-910719-97-8

Print management by Verité CM Ltd

www.veritecm.com

Printed in England

Contents

Introduction	1
Tackling the language problem	3
The 'E' word	4
We Have Everything We Need	5
People Resources	5
Other Resources	6
Looking Outwards	7
We are already doing our best!	7
How is the Process Delivered?	9
A Look at the Process	10
Some Examples	13
An Outreach in North Norfolk	13
A Small Church in East Sussex	15
A Midlands Church on the Edge of Closure	18

Introduction

What goes through your mind when you hear the words *mission* or *evangelism*? We know that in many rural churches just the mention of these words and people will be looking for the door. But can mission really be fun? I have spent a lifetime helping rural churches to grow through mission, and we offer help to any church concerned about decline or wanting to find new ways to serve their local community. We want more churches to discover that mission can be fun.

For the first 25 years of my ministry I combined being a minister of a church with being part of a specialist team that undertook short-term outreach programmes for rural churches of various denominations. While this was often exciting, there was a flaw in the strategy.

Imagine a team of four very skilled people coming to your village at the request of your church. They have talented singers and preachers, people gifted in working with young people and older people, gospel artists and storytellers. For two weeks they run activities each day in homes, in school, in the local pub, in the village hall and in church. It is all extremely exciting, but then they leave to work elsewhere.

The following Sunday things would be back to normal. The local clergyperson, possibly already overstretched, is left alone to lead the follow up. If what was 'normal' had not been attracting people in the past, it is unlikely the church will keep any new people that may have attended the outreach. There must be a better way!

I used to be part of just such a team ministry and, though it was very fruitful and enjoyable, I started to think through looking for a better way. It was this that gave rise to the concept of strategies carefully designed to fit comfortably with the limited resources typical in rural churches, and that are appropriate for both the church and the village culture. We called it a **"Tailored Mission Strategy".**

After all, if you were buying a new suit or costume and had the choice of selecting something off the peg or getting something specifically designed to your taste and shape, what would you choose? Get it right and you would feel comfortable wearing it on any occasion. This is how we approached *Tailored Mission Strategy.*

Years of experience living and working in all kinds of rural settings all over the UK, and experience from settled ministry in rural churches enabled us both to understand various rural contexts, and the constraints and opportunities, that lead to growth. University business studies provided insight into an approach that created sustainable development. This was the third and important element. So, how does it work?

Tackling the language problem

While the word *mission* can mean a venture or expedition, in this context it simply means *purpose*. Many churches have a mission statement. A Mission Statement is a succinct summary for the reason for existence.

You may have heard of the "Five Marks of Mission". They were developed by the Anglican Consultative Council back in 1984 and quickly won wide acceptance among Anglicans and other Christian traditions. They provide churches around the world a practical and memorable "checklist" for mission activities. They are not a final and complete statement on mission, but they offer a practical guide to the holistic nature of mission. They are a useful checklist for all churches that wish to share in God's mission (*Mission Dei*) They are:

1. To proclaim the Good News of the Kingdom
2. To teach, baptise and nurture new believers
3. To respond to human need by loving service
4. To transform unjust structures of society, to challenge violence of every kind and pursue peace and reconciliation
5. To strive to safeguard the integrity of creation, and sustain and renew the life of the earth

All Christians are invited to share in God's mission. Individually we might prioritise one or two of the five marks. However, every church should strive to incorporate all five, at least to some degree. But we are not in this alone. We have the fellowship of other churches and, supremely, we are assured of God's aid as we answer his call.

The 'E' word

The trouble with the word evangelism is that it carries significant images, and not all of these are good. You may have seen some bad examples that have made you cringe, but we should never allow bad examples to create a barrier to a healthy understanding.

The word is biblical and simply means sharing good news. So, if a practice is not good news then it is not truly evangelism. Intriguingly, the New Testament only includes the word evangelist three times, however, the phrase used in New Testament Greek (in which it was originally written) appears many times as sharing the good news or the message of the kingdom of God.

In *Tailoring Mission Strategies,* we never expect people to adapt to poor examples. We will always encourage better practices that enable us to understand evangelism in ways with which we can find ourselves comfortable.

We Have Everything We Need

God will never ask us to do anything beyond our ability given his help. In a rural mission conference, a church leader commented that his village church did not have what they needed to do what they wanted to do for God. A fellow clergyman replied, *"God has already given you everything you need in order to do what he is asking you to do right now"*

This profound statement draws on evidence from scripture and the rationale that a youth with a sling and stone was all a nation needed to save them from their enemies. A boy with a few small loaves and fish was all that was needed to feed five thousand and produce twelve baskets full of leftovers. In both situations it was God's help that made it possible.

If God has already given to each church everything they need in order to do what he is asking them to do right now, then it is important to see what we have got and seek to discern what it is he is asking us to do with it.

People Resources

Since God works with and through human beings, a good place to start is exploring who we have. God will use our personality, our natural gifts, our life experiences, and our connections. To these he often adds his own special gifts. It is not only clergy that have a vocation.

Most Christians believe that God has a particular purpose for each life. One of the most exciting experiences anyone can have is discovering that purpose. If this is true, as I believe it is, then within any church the combination of human resources might provide a clue as to what he is asking the church to do right now.

If there is anything more wonderful than discovering God's purpose in a Christian's life, it is being part of a church that has discovered a shared sense of purpose. It is revitalising and remains motivating.

Other Resources

Sometimes this takes a little thinking 'outside the box' to discover all the assets available. In my experience and in various situations these have included a farm, a tearoom, a pub, a piece of land, a shop, a deer park, and assorted private homes. When these were made available for the mission of a church, we saw amazing things.

Looking Outwards

Often in many rural churches the busyness of looking after their own needs means the thought of meeting the needs of others outside the church can seem overwhelming.

Surveys are useful. Sometimes, a simple question such as, "What can we do for you?" can reveal surprising answers that might just match the resources available.

In addition to discovering needs there are often opportunities that can be grasped. Sometimes needs and opportunities are combined.

Some churches create the impression that they are only interested in getting more people to swell the congregation and money to maintain historic buildings. It has been noted that when churches start to use their resources generously to respond to community needs, growth is often a consequence.

We are already doing our best!

We all feel this at times, and it may well be true. We are keen to affirm and encourage what is already being done.

The common school report comment, *"could do better!"* can sometimes become a tyranny. Such a comment is only of value if the resources needed to enable improvement are made available. What might be needed in the school context? Is more parental support needed?

Is there a need for more encouragement and affirming what is being achieved? Is the service of a classroom assistant needed? It might be any, all, or a combination of these factors that would help the student to do better.

I was uncertain at times as whether *"Could do better"* was a criticism of poor performance, or a revelation as to what was achievable beyond a good performance!

The life and work of many churches is being maintained by a few people who could easily become weary and find that a *'could do better'* exhortation sounds like *'could do more'*, which is the last thing they want to hear.

Rural clergy are often overstretched with additional responsibilities from multi-parish benefices in various forms or growing church circuits. Furthermore, they often find that they now face expectations for which they are untrained and unskilled, and far from what they expected in their vocation.

Undertaking a tailored mission process is not yet another layer of work. It is about releasing and refreshing. Mission should never be a burden, or awkward. It should be fun.

How is the Process Delivered?

Rural Mission Solutions offers a facilitator who will begin by carefully looking and listening to the people who make up the church that has invited our help. It would be foolish to make assumptions without taking care to understand the current situation and any aspirations that rise from the collective wisdom in the church.

What is especially important is that as many people as possible who make up the usual congregation share in the process. The process is just as important as any outcomes achieved. We try to make it a happy and encouraging experience for everyone.

You will find a few examples at the end of this booklet.

In the past, the process has been largely delivered at an Away Day or several Away Days. However, restrictions during the Covid-10 pandemic led to creating a series of six interactive webinars, held fortnightly. Some Webinars include practical applications or discussions in small groups. The webinars are led by an experienced Rural Mission Adviser and normally last around one hour.

The aim of the process is to enable a church to develop and implement strategies that they have designed themselves. We only facilitate the process.

A Look at the Process

The aim of the process is to help the church or other inviting body to develop and implement appropriate and effective mission strategies. These will be determined by the members of the church. The process is interactive, adapted to suit the local situation, and usually led by a facilitator. It is a journey that should always be undertaken with as many people as possible.

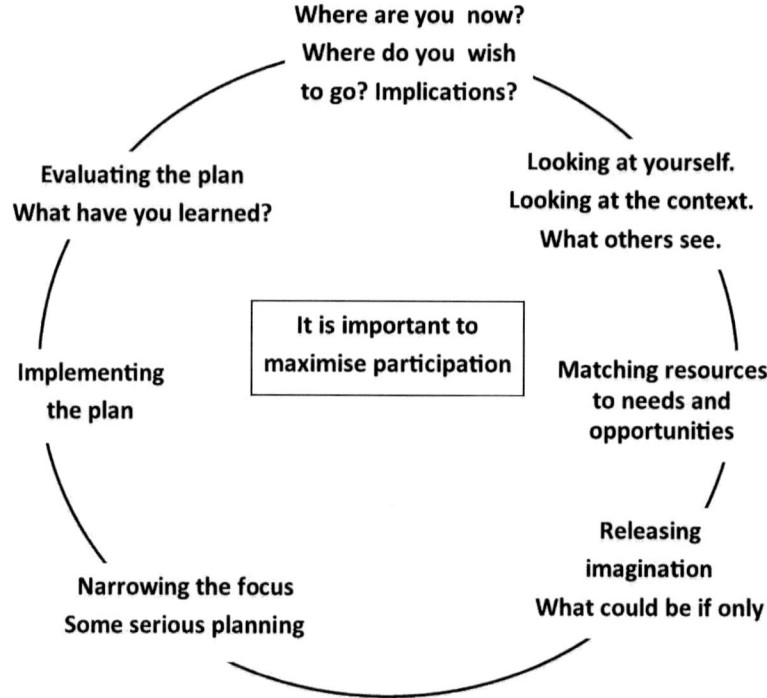

It starts with carefully understanding the current situation and the implication if nothing changes.

Is there a Mission Statement? What is its purpose? How is it working in practice? Are there specific problems? If so, can these be prioritised? We will also tackle the problem with the language of mission.

The next step is to undertake a process of looking more closely at the strengths and weaknesses of the church. We explore to see what resources we already have. We also explore together the opportunities and constraints within the wider community. There will be a video to watch and some mapping to do.

The third step builds on what has been learned and calls for a release of imagination. What actions might be undertaken to change the situation? All ideas are welcome, and nothing is rejected out of hand? Are we able to use any of our strengths to grasp opportunities? Are there any weaknesses that could be improved? Can we overcome any of the constraints? Are there any possible hazards to avoid?

The fourth step involves generating ideas for possible strategies, analysing these carefully and determining the most appropriate course of action, and creating a plan of action. By now we should have answered the *why* question, but there is the *what, how, who, where and when* questions to consider. Everyone will need to be of one mind, and know where their particular skills fit in.

The fifth step is implementation. Putting the plan into action.

The sixth step is evaluation. When this takes place will have been determined in step four. The church will also have determined the criteria for evaluating progress. It is also possible that there may have been other useful outcomes that were not expected.

The final step is to start the cycle all over again. Some things will have changed both for the church and the local community. It is important not to let the momentum lapse. Church life is not unlike trying to climb up a downward moving escalator. If we do not keep moving forward, we will eventually find ourselves slipping backwards.

Some Examples

It is an important ethical aspect of the work of Rural Mission Solutions that we guarantee anonymity. The following stories are shared with permission, but their precise location is not given.

An Outreach in North Norfolk

The request came not long after another colleague I had left an organisation that conducted short term outreaches for rural churches. It would be the first opportunity to put into practice the principles that now inform our work in *Rural Mission Solutions.* The invitation had come from an Anglican church that had never done anything like this previously and with which we had only a tenuous connection.

In the former organisation, the plan for the outreach would have been devised by the organisation and followed a set pattern. This was to be different. An Away-Day was arranged to enable the members of the core congregation to plan the programme for a ten-day outreach. We were offering a team of three people to support the outreach, but the emphasis was on the church to both plan and provide the resources.

They began by drawing a map of the village and locating where church members were living. They also undertook a simple social analysis to help us understand the local culture. Then they listed the resources of the church, its members, and their skills.

One Church Warden owned a Deer Farm that was open to visitors, so the church chose to use this for the opening event on a Saturday to which the whole village was invited. There were trips around the farm, a barbecue, some folk singing, and a fancy-dress competition based on characters in the Bible.

It was well attended, and the fancy dress competition provided an interesting opportunity to talk about each entrant which included the vicar and the other church warden as Balaam's ass! It was fun and demonstrated that what would be taking place was not threatening. One of the aims for the outreach that the church had identified was engaging with young families. They certainly achieved that.

The following day, the bishop attended the morning service and commissioned the team. Unsurprisingly, there was a larger than usual congregation. These two events served to raise the profile for the seven days that would follow. These included a series of coffee mornings in various homes throughout the village to which neighbours were invited, a senior citizens' lunch, a men's breakfast in the village pub, and a musical concert supported by a talented choir from the nearby Methodist Church.

As the days went by, we were able to tick off each of the aims the church members had identified when planning the outreach. At each event, a friendly and simple explanation of the gospel was given, and people were invited to take away attractive copies of the Gospel of John that incorporated a simple prayer of response to Jesus. The discussions at the coffee mornings enabled the hosts to say something about their faith with their neighbours and many copies of the gospel were taken. Though they had never done anything like this before, and lacked confidence, the visiting team was amazed as we watched and listened. We almost felt redundant!

The nine days concluded with a Family Service which saw the Parish Church packed, with many indicating that during the week they had taken a step forward in faith - some for the first time.

The Outreach the church had designed aimed to share the gospel with people who lived in specific areas of the village, it aimed to build the church's relationship with young families, it aimed to reach men and older people in the village, and it hoped to grow the church. It was their programme, based on recognising needs and opportunities in the community and using the resources immediately available. It achieved all that they had hoped.

A Small Church in East Sussex

Not long after this initial opportunity to test the principles of a tailored mission approach, an independent village church faced with a crisis asked for help. The congregation had declined and was now in single figures and apart from one young farming family most of the others were retired. A few Christians living in the village were commuting to a new charismatic church in a town some eight miles away. That church had offered to take over the village chapel or alternatively to plant a new church in the village. They needed help.

The village had a population of 1,000 divided between two distinct communities. A further 1,000 lived in three small hamlets nearby. There was no church building in the main part of the village. The chapel was situated on a lane just outside the main housing area, and the Parish Church was situated half a mile beyond that.

Some *tailored mission* research revealed several weaknesses. Church services were led by lay preachers on a list of twenty people who conducted the services in various styles. There was no consistency or continuity. The church had little engagement with the village community. Worse still was that many in the village were unaware that it existed. Those that were aware of it did not consider it relevant and held a poor opinion of it.

The church members had indicated a readiness to change, so a programme was commenced that addressed the weaknesses. The list of twenty lay preachers was reduced to a team of four who would conduct their ministry in the same style using common material and contemporary language.

During a visitation programme to raise awareness of the chapel, a young Christian family was discovered who had moved into the village the day before. Not long afterwards, another young Christian family, new to the village, was discovered. Within a relatively short period of time, the average age of the congregation had reduced, and the children's work had grown from two to six. The culture of the church also changed, becoming more welcoming and friendly, offering coffee and other refreshments after the service (that was a radical change). Others began to be attracted.

The strengths and skills within the church had also changed. There were now opportunities to work with the village school and the young mums in the church were networking with others at the school gate. Holding a Holiday Bible Club became a possibility.

Other opportunities were soon discovered. In one of the nearby hamlets there was a specialist college run by a Christian couple. Having been attracted to the new life at the chapel, this brought a few young men and women. It also offered a venue with a swimming pool. That combined with the ability to hold a barbecue in one of the farm barns created further scope to match the strengths of the church to the opportunities in the village.

Over the years that followed the Sunday morning congregation grew to around fifty plus a separate youth congregation of around a dozen. A fresh expression of church (cafe style) was introduced once a month in a new village hall, the church was asked to run the village youth club, three young people engaged in overseas mission work, a good partnership with the Parish Church was developed, and a closed shop in the village was opened as an information centre and drop-in resource for the community that was originally run by the church and later gifted to the Parish Council.

The church had developed an effective missional culture through an ongoing process of exploring needs and opportunities to serve the community and seeking to match them from the resources available to the church.

A Midlands Church on the Edge of Closure

This church is situated in the East Midlands. It had slowly declined over several decades and had more than its share of ups and downs. It had two members with one service a month. The village in which it was situated was on a relatively quiet B-road. The population was just over 700 at the time of our engagement. The church was a historic Congregational church with roots going back to 1662 and located in the centre of the village. A community survey had revealed a need for a venue for a Youth 'Drop-In'. To accommodate this the central aisle of pews had been removed to allow activities.

There were two other churches in this small village. The Parish Church, which was located on a hill at one end of the village was part of a multi-parish benefice incorporating churches in three villages, and two small hamlets. The vicar who lived in a neighbouring village was evangelical and mission minded but held to the view that the Anglican Church was the primary denomination and not particularly ecumenical.

The Roman Catholic Church was a simple timber structure. Almost all its congregation came from beyond the village with some even travelling from a town some distance from the church. The priest lived in that town and was only seen coming to take Mass on Sundays.

In the village where the Anglican priest lived there was a small United Reformed Church, and in the third village was a small and conservative Independent Evangelical Chapel, mostly supported by commuters from the town.

It would have been easy to argue that perhaps the Congregational Church should close, but might it have a lively future serving the local community? The review process noted that its location in the village was a strength. Another strength was the awareness of impending death! Change would be possible. If it were to have a future, it would need to develop an identity distinct from other churches in the area but taking care not to undermine the life of the Parish Church. The Community Survey had created a degree of sympathy from the wider village community. Implementing any changes would be easy as in a Congregational church financial responsibility and all decisions were made by the congregation.

Apart from providing some consistent ministry (even if supplied from a distance) other opportunities came from its location and the sympathy from the wider community.

From the start, the ethos of the church was to serve the local community. It was a church in the heart of the village and developed as a church with the village in its heart. It was happy to make its premises available to the community free of charge for anything that benefitted the village. During the Covid-19 pandemic, technical skills in this church enabled setting up joint live online services for all the local churches.

Ignoring its own financial needs, it hosted community events and raised funds for a village adopted charity. Its self-denial and generosity did not go unnoticed. Attendances and membership grew to around twenty, almost all from the local village.

Instead of defining itself doctrinally, as the Independent Church and the Parish Church did, instead it used a statement of values based on the teaching of Jesus, and with which non-believers were able to identify.

Visitors would comment, *"You are very normal here!"* as they found themselves met with good hospitality. It became the go to church for funerals. Its own demise once threatened, it continues as a thriving village church.